**OF
THIS
AND
THAT**

*a very
human
experience*

Karen Sandford-Albarda

 FriesenPress

Suite 300 - 990 Fort St
Victoria, BC, Canada, V8V 3K2
www.friesenpress.com

Copyright © 2021 by Karen Sandford-Albarda
First Edition — 2021

All rights reserved.

No part of this publication may be reproduced in any form, or by any means, electronic or mechanical, including photocopying, recording, or any information browsing, storage, or retrieval system, without permission in writing from FriesenPress.

ISBN
978-1-03-910352-8 (Hardcover)
978-1-03-910351-1 (Paperback)
978-1-03-910353-5 (eBook)

1. Poetry

Distributed to the trade by The Ingram Book Company

Reaching deep
into my heart
and
weaving my feelings
and my words
into
one.

CONTENTS

1.	Uninspired
3	Lost
5	A Painter
7	Finding Me
9	A Friend
11	Words
13	My Credo
15	An Analogy
17	A Circle In The Night
19	Silence
21	Sleep
23	To My Love
25	You Are You
27	Ashes In The Lake
29	Anger
31	Cancer *Or* I Am So Angry
35	Retirement

37	. . . .	Just A Thought
39	. . . .	About You And Me
41	. . . .	The Second Wife
43	. . . .	Faces
45	. . . .	This Face
49	. . . .	It's All About Aging
53	. . . .	The Chain Of Life
55	. . . .	Cry With Me
57	. . . .	The End Of A Life
59	. . . .	I Had A Brother
61	. . . .	Life In Pieces
69	. . . .	Just Passing Through
73	. . . .	Country Mouse To City Mouse.
75	. . . .	Goodbye To My Sadie
77	. . . .	Still

UNINSPIRED

When your brain feels
                empty
and you are feeling
                uninspired
where do you go?
How do you get the magic back?
Moments of pure inspiration
are infrequent.
The in-between is
                excruciating.

LOST

I am in transition.
I am hopelessly lost
              within myself.

Or......
Am I searching for something
      and have stepped out of myself?
Where do I go from here?

Much left to say.
Much left to understand.

Now,
taking time out
until
the words come back to me.

A PAINTER

I have become disassembled.
I know what the pieces are
but not how to put them back together
                                                again.
I admire those who know
what their lives are supposed to look like.
I don't know,
        for right now
I cannot see it.
The big white canvas is blank.
Where to begin?
When will the tip of the paintbrush
                      be brave enough
                      to touch the canvas again?

It is such a big blank canvas.

FINDING ME

I'm going to muster up
        my courage
        and
        gather up the pieces
that once were a part of me.
I will choose only the best ones,
the ones that made me proud.
I will put myself
        back together
and find happiness again.

A FRIEND

You and I are great friends.
We are the same
              but different.
It's in the sameness
we find our friendship.
In our differences
we find our support.
We need each other
as we figure out how to navigate
              this incredible new journey.

WORDS

There is a consequence
        to each and every word
        that comes
        from your mouth.
For.......
Words can destroy you.
Words can lift you up
                and make you all you can be
                and more.
Words have the power to make you feel
                      loved
                      or
                      rejected
        for the power of the tongue is great.
Choose your words with care.
The word that escapes becomes a free spirit.
It can never come back.
Live out loud
but speak gently and touch a heart
                in the best way possible.
Speak and create the diaphanous bridge
                from mind to mind.
My words are my truths.
Please hear them
        for they are pieces of my soul.

MY CREDO

The truth
is like the umbrella
over everything!
Without the truth
            nothing
                  matters.
Nothing has any value
                      without the umbrella.

AN ANALOGY

I am a beach pebble.
    A simple stone in the sand.
I have been tossed
    and thrown by the waves.
From time to time
    I was loved for a moment, then cast
    rejected
        back into the water.
Oh so slowly
    my corners were worn off.
Oh so slowly
    I became smooth and rounded.
I have a shape.
My own shape.
Now I am exactly how I was meant to be.
Sometimes
    I am held and loved.
    Treasured.
For now,
    I am perfect.

A CIRCLE IN THE NIGHT

Here I am again......
Awake
instead of asleep.
Going round and round
           in my mind.
Same old story,
      story without end.
The story is a circle.
Same story as yesterday.
I lie in the dark
           alone.
A solitary being
           in the universe,
alone with my story
and no end in sight.
Tomorrow, in the dark
I will do it again,
           same story,
this story that has no answer.

SILENCE

In the inky black of the night
      so softly
you wrap yourself around my head
            like cotton wool.
      At times
your presence becomes deafening,
      at times
even frightening.
I become aware of
      a vast empty space
      and my aloneness.
      At times
you hurt my ears
and then,
      alone with my thoughts
I become the observer of my mind's restlessness
as it curls up around life's endless question marks.

In a few short hours you will leave me again,
the silence will retreat
and I will be thrust
          back into the chaos
          and the noise of life,
the never-ending discord of humanity.

SLEEP

Ever elusive.......
      lying here beside you,
      sleep evades me.
      My love.
You are at peace.
How quietly you breathe......
                      in and out
                      and in again.
Oh, please don't stop!
I try to breathe in unison,
      but I cannot.
My rhythm is slower.
I am lost in my aloneness,
      lying here in the blue black silence
      of this night.
I touch your body
      for I must know you are still there.
I want the comforting warmth
                      of you.
When you slipped into your dream
      did you take me with you?
I hold your hand between my breasts
      for I need you to feel my heart.
The heart that now belongs to you.

TO MY LOVE

I blew here on the wind.
I am but a small bird
      flying solo in this world.
If you want to hold me in your hand
be careful
for I am fragile.
I feel
everything.
Only my weightless feathers
              can protect me
              from how you handle me.
And
You alone
      can make me sing.

YOU ARE YOU

What your ancestors did
                    is not you.
What the people in your life did
                    is not you.
You are you.
You are your values and beliefs.
You have earned your own place.
That is all.
I know the you.
      It is the you
               I love.

ASHES IN THE LAKE

This day
      is the day,
      the time,
your beloved mother's ashes
      will come to rest in the lake.
Your family by your side.
You will be enveloped in your sadness.
I am not there
      But......
my thoughts will be with you.
I too will be sad.

You will forever miss her love.
Still......
In your life
        you will be loved.
Now......
by another woman,
        for I will love you.
Somewhere along the way,
        you stole my heart.
I think......
Your mother knew.

ANGER

The pain bubbles up
and turns into
                anger.
Anger that carries with it
unbearable shame.
But, my anger is nothing but
                frustration.
Frustration because you do not understand my pain.
Words come from me,
      words I do not want to say.
They are not
              Me.
And yet they are.
They come from someone I don't know.
Someone I have not known before.
The pain is there
            deep inside me.
Each day we add to it
      we are building a tower.
The tower will topple.
                    And so will I.

CANCER OR I AM SO ANGRY

This is to all the well-intentioned people
who do amazing things
      for people with cancer.
You congratulate yourselves
            for your riding
            for your running.
But……
You don't have any idea how it feels
      to have cancer.
You cannot possibly know
      if you haven't done it yet.
May you never know!

You don't know how it feels to have a body
      out of control.
A body that let you down.
A body you cannot trust.
            Ever again.
Don't paint me,
    dance for me,
    walk for me,
    or replacc my precious curls.
You cannot know how it feels
      if you haven't done it yet.
May you never know!

Be by my side.
Don't make me take this journey
                  Alone!
While I agree to be poisoned.
While I agree to insult my body.
Sit by me.
For,
I am frightened for my life.

Be gentle with me.
For,
I have never needed you more.
Even then,
you cannot truly know how it feels
        if you haven't done it yet.
    May you never know!

RETIREMENT

Today......
      Both a beginning
      and an ending.
This most important of all days!
You will step away from the known.
You will become creative
and have the luxury of time
                to dream a dream.
                Many dreams perhaps.
You will create a new story.
You will create a new you.
      A you, you didn't know before.
Limitless possibilities!
Dream and discover all you were meant to be.
I will be by your side
         to watch the unfolding.
You won't be alone.

JUST A THOUGHT

If……
I had found the right person.
The person to share my life journey
      and
I thought that I had.
The person I love with all that I am.
Why should it be so hard?

You wanted a companion.
The universe listened
          and gave me to you.
    But……
To have a companion
you must be a companion.
    Otherwise …….
You have nothing,
          only yourself.

ABOUT YOU AND ME

Dressed in their overcoats
            they walked by the lake.
They talked of kings
        and queens
        and important things
        and changing this broken world.
Always in overcoats,
this man and this woman.
Then,
    very slowly
the sun began to shine.
It peeked out at the man and the woman
            and it began to shine.
The overcoats melted away.
The man and the woman changed.
The man became a boy.
The woman became a little girl.
A boy and a girl masquerading in overcoats
            as a man,
            as a woman.
A man and a woman no more.

THE SECOND WIFE

You shared your bed with her.
You are asking me to look at her
                                      and never think of that.
You share your bed with me and
you are asking me to feel
                          special.

You created new life with her.
You are asking me to look at her
                                      and never think of that.
You share your bed with me and
you are asking me to feel
                          special.

You are asking me to share you,
                                  my love,
                          with her.
You share your bed with me and
you are asking me to feel
                          special.

You are asking too much of me.

FACES

Today I looked at myself
and
I look awful!
I am thinking......
Here is the lesson.
    Don't judge the way someone looks.
    Don't think they haven't tried
                      as hard as they should.
Today my spirit can't shine through.
My energy has left me.
Today
I look awful
    and it's alright.

THIS FACE

I look at this face,
        my face.
On what day did it become so complicated?
When it was new,
        so many stories ago,
it had a perfect mouth
it had a perfect nose
it had two eyes
        like clear deep pools of wonder.
        Innocence
        Anticipation
The new face with smooth skin,
      pulled tight over a perfect frame.
Colour like alabaster
     with just a hint of pink.
Perfection!
Somewhere along the way
          it became complicated,
          this face.
So complicated!
The skin no longer fits.
     It is too big.
Sagging and wrinkled from too much life.
Deeply etched creases
         from too many smiles,
         from too much sorrow.
No longer alabaster……
     too much rain
     too much sun
     too much wind
The eyes are now knowing eyes……

       eyes of great love
       eyes of sadness
       eyes of a long life lived

This face has become complicated!

IT'S ALL ABOUT AGING

We may mourn the loss of the person
                we once were.
Perhaps,
we did not honour her enough.
Once long ago
    we did not see
    how perfect we were.
Endless years ahead of us!
Of course
we would stay the same
    for
weren't we timeless?
Our bodies would continue to do
        as we told them to.
    But……
    We have aged!
The end is much closer than we think.
We look in the mirror
        and we see our mothers.
Barely recognizing ourselves
and accepting who we have become.
In our minds
this is not how we see ourselves.
On the outside
we wear the stories of our lives
like a badge of having survived it all.
It is called
    character.
On the inside
    we have become beautiful.
Often wise and compassionate
    because of all we have learned on this journey.

We have learned to love
                        the many kinds of love.
One day
much too soon
this extraordinary journey will be over.

THE CHAIN OF LIFE

I have lived a life.
A life of countless textures.
A life with many chapters
      each with a beginning and an ending.
I once thought of life as infinite.
Now I know it is finite
            for my body is telling me so.
Today becomes one more gift.
Can I remember to treat it as one?
Each day is precious
        singular
        one of a kind.
I think I have become Me.
I think I am at peace with Me.
The pieces are coming together
        and I have an understanding
of how it all fits.
As I look over my shoulder
        each chapter becomes smaller
and
        each carries with it a purpose
                a lesson.
The lessons all strung together
     have made me Me.

CRY WITH ME

I look at our broken world.
A thousand tears bubble
                so close to the surface.
Cry with me.

I look at our broken world.
Why are those tears
           poised to overflow?
Cry with me.

I look at our broken world.
Why is there such sadness
             living within me?
Cry with me.

I look at our broken world.
Why did I save these tears
               for the end of my lifetime?
Cry with me.

I look at our broken world
and the depth of my feeling
            is too big
           for me.
Come cry with me.

THE END OF A LIFE

The uncertainty of it all.
Will I get more life
       or
will this be the end of my story?
What I do know is……
       Make it count.
Be all you know how to be.
See all you know how to see.
The wonder of life
            in this miraculous place.
This is the biggest lesson of all.
Let me live it with dignity
          compassion
          and gentleness.

I HAD A BROTHER

You were born to a woman
     who did not like men
     so much.
Did you already know that?
Did you already feel that

     when you were just becoming a human being?
        Or......
Why were you so mad?
Is that the reason?
     Of course it was.
How hurtful for you!
I was already waiting for you,
your sibling of the opposite sex.
I was always in your way.
     No need!
There was lots of space between us.
     You were you.
     I was myself.
Slowly, I became the villain in the stories
        you created in your mind.
I tried to speak with you.
You always read between the lines.
     But the spaces between the lines
        were empty.
Why could you not see that?
Each time I accomplished something
        you liked me less.
Now you have gone
     and I am sad.
We were so the same
     but so different.

Gone forever is the chance to understand each other.

LIFE IN PIECES

Once I was a child.
I learned to play,
          to live in my imagination.
I heard music
          and music became me.
I was molded.
I was protected and kept safe
          in the horrors of war.
I had rules.
     Many rules.
I was corrected or praised.
I tried to be good,
          very very good.
Not always good enough.
I had a soul.
An old soul.

I became a sister.
A halo of beautiful golden curls,
his tiny fists clenched tight in anger.
I learned about jealousy.
        Not mine, but his.
In my innocence
      I could not see the reason.

In my mature years
    still I could not see the reason.
We were each perfect.
We each had our place
           in the family
           in the world.
Jealousy for a lifetime.
          His lifetime.
I had a soul.

I became an adult.
All too soon
    I became a wife.
I tried to please,
    make all things perfect.
I had dreamed a dream.
Always creative and it saved me.
A marriage in two pieces,
    the second so much better than the first.
I learned a lot
        as I grew up.
I had a soul.

I became a mother.
My life became joy.
How I loved those small people
    as I learned who they were.
I watched them grow.
Who would they become?
They filled my life.
        They did not disappoint.
I had a soul.

I became a daughter.
A daughter-mother.
Suddenly,
    I was needed.
    A friend to my mother.
I learned who I was to her.
I learned who I had been to her.
At last,
    before it was too late
I learned that she loved me.
    I had waited a lifetime.
        She left me.
I had a soul.

I had cancer.
I became nothing.
I was taken apart and
      put back together again.

I was poked and prodded and poisoned.
I was nobody.
I existed.
I was quiet.
        Silence!
But still,
      somewhere in there
I had a soul.

I became a widow.
I learned
      I could do all things by myself.
I learned who I was,
      who I always had been.
I learned I was loved.
I was reminded of great joy
          and how that had once felt.
I found happiness in who I was.
I was myself.
I was truth.
I had a soul.

I was a friend.
Slowly,
      oh so slowly
my friend became my love.
I had expectations.
But..............
Our expectations were not the same.
We had lived a long life.
We were who we had become
            in life's journey.

In this love
                I got lost along the way.
                I lost myself.
But...........
I am still truth.
I have a soul.

My soul is big,
the flame hasn't gone out.
I will be back.

JUST PASSING THROUGH

Lately
      I am asking myself......
What's it like to die?
What will it be like
              not
              to be?
And ....
Does the world cease to exist
              if I'm not there?
In that case
      is life an illusion?
Is this whole magnificent journey
                  an illusion?
Did I create it with my mind?
When I die......
        Will it be the end of me?
Will I dissolve into a vast
           black
              empty space?
Should I be afraid?
What is it like to die?
Or......

Will I come back to a different world?
Life unending.
Who will I be?
Will I be me,
      but richer for all I have learned?
Will I still know you when I meet you?
Will you still know me?
Will it be to this world
              but at a new time?
Will this world have learned
          to be a better world?

Will we have learned
                       to treat it with more respect?
Will we be in awe of its beauty?

What is it like to die?

COUNTRY MOUSE TO CITY MOUSE.

I once looked at the sky.
Beautiful white puffy clouds
                                        floating.
I watched through the pine trees
while smelling the forest.
Oh glorious silence!
And I thought.......
        This must be like heaven!

Now
    I look at the sky
Beautiful white puffy clouds
                                        floating.
I watch through masses of wires.
I smell fumes all around me
and hear never-ending sounds
                          of human activity.
Still, the clouds stay the same.
        This is not heaven!

The butterflies dance
and notice only the flowers.

GOODBYE TO MY SADIE

On that terrible morning
even though you were in pain,
you wagged your tail
                when you saw me.
Those knowing brown eyes
looked at me
                with love
                as they always had.
You trusted me to care for you.
Now, I was asked to play god.
I knelt on the floor
beside you.
I softly held your beautiful head
                in my hands,
                one last time.
I kissed your warm velvet ears.
You closed your eyes
                and you left this earth.
                    In peace.
You had always known how much I loved you.

Somehow,
I will have to learn to live without you.

STILL

My world is still beautiful
when I remember to think like a child.
        Simple,
           but so beautiful.
All creatures here by accident.
                              All the same
                              All with purpose
                              All inherently good
We share our miraculous planet.
                              Our home.
In my world
I still see things in black and white.
In my world
two and two are still four.
In my world
right and wrong still exist
        and I still know the difference.
How could the world try to be ugly
        when there is still such beautiful music?
I am happy I still know where I am
        when I remember to think like a child.
It is the child in me
        who still sees the world as beautiful
and
        still sees the possibility of peace on earth.

CPSIA information can be obtained
at www.ICGtesting.com
Printed in the USA
LVHW080152110521
687078LV00002B/192